"What barrier is there that love cannot break?"

-Ghandi

© Little Boy Press 2020

Amsterdam

All of the designs in the book were by made by the author while she had nice homemade food alongside her dog amelie in a beautiful quiet atelier. No writers or illustrators were harmed in the making of this book.

For more information, visit www.coloringmethod.com

Daily Self-Blessings:

Simple Coloring Meditations for Inner-Kindness

The coloring book for meditating simply and anywhere you are.

Amsterdam

Preface

Wherever you are sitting, wherever you are standing right now, take this moment to connect to the presence of your body in the space where you are. Feel the materials in contact with you, be it the hardness of a wooden chair, the softness of a gentle throw, or the flexibility of a patch of grass. Take a brief moment to listen to the sounds, near and far, delicate or boisterous, dreamy or rugged. Tune into the spaces of silence, nigh and distant, long or precise, hushed or vivid. Dwell in this space of awareness, savoring the essence of the air, be it moist or dry, sweet or bitter, intense, or yielding. And as you relate to your environment, interacting with your senses one by one, remember this essential truth, — You are connected.

A large part of embracing and working through this connection, rather than against it, is to soundly consider that whatever is happening inside of you is connected to what is happening outside of you and inside of others. This might seem somewhat like an intricate interpretation of a complex and distant philosophical concept, but it actually comes down to the core foundation of earthly existence: we are all linked together. The factuality of interconnection can be approached through many avenues, including scientific findings in the fields of: physics, neuroscience, natural science, environmental cycles systems, epidemiology, social sciences such as sociology, psychology and geography et al. All of these fields utterly prove that the earth's interrelated environment bespeaks of the necessity to tend for each other and the world that we inhabit. This is the case since we are not as distant from one another or as disassociated from our environment as it may sometimes seem to be.

Through an extensive body of knowledge on the inherent natural systems of interconnection and interdependence, these evidence-based fields substantiate and uphold the importance of spiritual teachings and mindfulness-based practices rooted in cultivating values that nurture harmonious relationships, loving-kindness, empathy, and compassion.

These set of ideals form the basis of spiritual and philosophical teachings and practices such as loving-kindness and compassion-based meditations, which advocate for the personal and societal well-being through caring and wholehearted presence. These meditative practices approach mindfulness in a distinct way to other forms of awareness-building methods, as the use of prayer, blessing, and sacred acknowledgment are all useful tools that can be used to arrive at a more conscious state of being.

Developing a conscious relationship of respect and warm-heartedness with oneself and with the rest of the world, opens the way to transform constant feelings of separation and apprehension, into a holistic way of being of presence, harmony, and flow. The simple daily loving-kindness exercises found in this workbook have been crafted and curated so you can approach mindfulness practices with ease and focus, allowing you to implement the theory with practice.

Through blessing and loving-kindness exercises, your trust will grow as you tap into boundless internal energy capable of infinite self-worth, satisfaction, and meaningful relationships. The cultivation of benevolence will allow you to model your perception of reality to be one based on love rather than othering and action rather than reaction. This personal and collective shift can prove to be a compelling force in fostering mutual kindness and humanity amongst all.

Table of Contents

Introduction

The practice of self-blessing is recognizing oneself as a valuable, self-worthy, well-deserving individual. Self-Blessing is an exercise on self-compassion, loving-kindness, and inner-work. Blessing oneself is observing, perceiving, and remembering one's bearing and inner power. Self-blessing is explorative, inquisitive, and cathartic. Self-blessing is a knock in one's soul that answers. Self-blessing is presence in the infinite space and time continuum. Self-blessing is powerful. It is a guiding force to recognize oneself through one's humanity. Self-blessing says -I'm here for you, and I accept you, just as you are. Self-blessing is boundless and inexhaustible. Self-blessing heals. Self-blessing brings beauty and truth forth. Self-blessing is that unconditional and undivided nurturing self-love. Self-blessing is courageous, honest, straightforward, and undiluted. Self-blessing is transformational, as it allows one to recollect and reconnect with the sacredness of human existence.

Blessing yourself is one of the most valuable habits you can nurture as a way of inviting inner kindness into your life. Self-blessing comes down to the foundational act of cultivating benevolence towards yourself by intentionally well-wishing words of understanding through the use of simple actions, loving prayers, phrases, or affirmations. These small deeds are potent tools for cultivating self-love as they open the way for establishing a loving relationship with yourself based on loving-kindness.

Self-blessing is a powerful act as it leads the way for deep transformational inner-work. Blessing yourself opens an inner-dialog with your richly inner-world and your relation with your external projections. This introspective experience is grounded on the natural process of self-inquiry that arises by way of engaging and understanding your inner relation. Connecting with your inner world through loving-kindness can bring clarity with the ways that you speak to yourself, motivate yourself and mentally move through your identity, bringing forth: empowerment, sensibility, and a strong sense of self-compassion.

Inner loving-kindness goes a long way, as the way that you feel, communicate, and treat yourself is directly linked to the way that other people engage and connect with you. Moreover, the key to be able to extend benevolence and goodwill to others is to start with yourself first and then to spread this love to others.

On the Benefits of Self-Blessing

Practicing loving-kindness through self-blessing has been directly linked with heightened levels of gratitude, a state that comes accompanied by elevated feelings of contentment, hope, and an overall sensation of positivity. The cultivation of gratitude through self-blessing and an appreciative mindset has been scientifically proven to have positive effects on an individual's social, emotional, physical, and personal well-being[1].

The research field of positive psychology, which is concerned with investigating human fulfillment and the aspects that improve the quality of life, substantiate that "gratitude is strongly and consistently associated with happiness."[2] This is the case since an attitude of gratitude has shown to decrease levels of stress, improving resilience to life's adversities and enriching social connections, as well as lessening feelings of isolation[3]. Moreover, employing gratitude based practices such as self-blessing, praying, and journaling has been shown to improve health indicators such as speeding recovery from a health setback[4], fewer symptoms of physical illness, and improvement of cognitive function[5] and mental health.

Such personal and interpersonal benefits reiterate the value of self-blessing as a mindfulness tool that can be used as a daily reflective practice. These scientific findings prove that through conscious effort and single focus engagement in these contemplative practices, it is possible to use self-blessing and gratitude to arrive at a more mindful and positive mental state of being[6].*

---

*Endnotes + more resources on the benefits of loving-kindness meditation can be found at the end of the book.

Notes on Self-Blessing

Self-blessing or cultivating benevolence towards oneself is a meditative tool that has been used throughout time by different cultures and spiritual traditions to invoke feelings of kindheartedness and compassion. These nurturing and gratitude-based practices occupy an essential role in the dogma of many of the world's religions, including Jewish, Christian, Muslim, Buddhist, Hindu, Shamanic, and Animistic cosmology and theology.

For mystical and animistic-based spiritual traditions, this holds true as, through this mythos, the divine is seen and felt throughout everything, including in oneself. In this sense, embracing the divine is a way of acknowledging and connecting with the grandeur and magical continuation of the universe. To connect with this divine is to appreciate, respect, and contemplate the beauty of existence, a practice that can be profound as it can change the way that one relates to every little thing and oneself.

In the mindfulness sphere of the present day, Metta or Loving-Kindness meditation, also known as Heart Opening meditation, is used as a way of engaging with contemplative blessing practices. This form of meditation employs both prayer and visualization to cultivate amity, love, and presence. Metta meditation comes from the Buddhist Theravada tradition and has been adapted to modern-day practices in mindfulness circles to be used by people regardless of their religion.

The foundation of Metta meditation is to first develop goodwill to oneself, then to loved ones, then to neutral ones, then to difficult ones or those who cause suffering, and finally to all sentient beings. Practicing loving-kindness can also be extended to blessing emotions, spaces, the elements, the trees, and nature as it is done through nature worshiping practices entrenched in numerous indigenous customs and sacred ceremonies throughout the world.

About the Blessings Library

The *Blessings Library* consists of mindfulness-based workbooks exploring simple yet powerful exercises to cultivate benevolence, amity, kindness, and interconnection. The Coloring Method workbooks of the Blessings Library have been crafted to create a safe and committed space for practicing the powerful act of blessing. These workbooks facilitate the practice and embodiment of loving-kindness and compassion through the open, supportive, and playful medium of coloring.

Each book contemplates a different blessing subject, be it through the blessing of oneself, the blessing of loved ones, the blessing of difficult ones, and the blessing of more abstract, spiritual, or collective themes such as the blessing of the countries and the blessing of the elements of nature. Moreover, in this Library, you will be able to find Metta meditations, Ho'oponopono meditations, and compassion-based meditations that focus on simple daily prayer exercises through the use of single-mindedness practice.

The Coloring Method *Blessing Workbooks* are meditation guides that deepen and enrich the act of blessing through the use of visualized and single-focus exercises based on simple imagery and potent oratory engaging activities. Each book contains a small number of guided prayers, affirmations, or blessings that can be repeated either audibly or mentally to connect with the intent of the practice. In the following pages, you will find a simple exploration of how you can develop and manifest your blessing practice with the aid of the simple guidelines from the Coloring Method.

The Coloring Method + The Act of Blessing

Developing Your Practice
Through the Coloring Method

The Coloring Method is a mindfulness tool used for establishing conscious presence by incorporating awareness-based practices with single-point concentration. This attentive form of single-mindedness, which is called samadhi in eastern philosophical thought, is a form of engaging with meditative practices and can be easily facilitated through contemplative arts such as coloring.

In this workbook, you will be using samadhi, or single-point concentration, to place your energy and focus on the act of blessing. To do this, you will be using the Coloring Method's simple three-step process of: Breath + Thought & Intention + Coloring Action. This simple process will aid you in gaining presence through breath as you direct your thought, blessing, and intention into the coloring of the given subject provided in the workbook.

Instructions

The suggested instructions are as follows: through the coloring of the appointed illustrated subject, you will be using your breath, intention, and blessing to focus on manifesting your purpose through action.

On this journey:

You will use your breath to find presence.

You will use your blessing to manifest loving-kindness and compassion.

You will use the act of coloring to gain mental focus and energize your message.

Breath and Presence

The act of breathing constantly brings life into the body, energizing every cell with oxygen, the basis of life. For this reason, when one brings awareness to the life force, one brings awareness to presence and being.

In the following Coloring Method exercises, you will be able to use your breath as a vehicle to bring consciousness into the now, as concentrating on your breathing will allow you to tune into your body and your presence.

Bringing consciousness into your breath is just as simple as bringing awareness to your inhalation and exhalation. Below you will find a simple breathing exercise to connect with your breath.

Practice

Sit in a comfortable and quiet space, and close your eyes. Begin to listen to your breath, without controlling it or judging it; just let it be. Once you are in touch with your breathing cycle, begin to feel how it manifests physically in your body. When you inhale, feel how your abdomen expands as you breath in and then on an exhale feel how your belly deflates as it let goes off all the air inside. To get more in touch with how this process happens, you can place the palm of your hand on your abdominal region and feel your body inhaling as it expands and exhaling as the belly slowly empties the air. Do this for a couple of minutes and feel how it feels to be with your breath.

Once you have tried this simple breathing exercise, you can bring this practice into an active meditation method, by synchronizing your breath with your movement. In the coloring method, you will be doing this by inhaling slowly and exhaling slowly as you color your intended subject below and convey your blessing. For this exercise, you will be coloring the shape of the human inside the circle as a way of relating to yourself.

Repeat this breath.blessing.coloring technique as many times as you need to until you are done with coloring the subject at hand and then continue unto the next illustration.

While doing this exercise, concentrate on your breath, your blessing or intention, and the act of coloring. The point of breathwork is to feel present within yourself, which will allow you to maintain your awareness at the moment and your meditative intention.

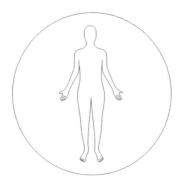

Recommendations

Creating a Safe Space for Your Meditation Practice

There are simple things you can do to create a safe space where you can feel comfortable and at ease before you start your meditation practice. This can be done in different ways and can include: using your favorite essential oil, wearing comfy clothes, having something "cozy" with you such as your favorite blanket, pillow, or a lovely cup of tea. Doing this will permit you to feel safe and present, allowing you to reconnect with the nurturing and loving-kindness aspects of yourself. Moreover, if it calls you, you can also ceremonially open a meditation space by using simple elements such as playing a bell, washing your hands, burning sacred smoke, or through any other ritual that personally calls you.

Call Presence through Breath

Allow yourself to arrive at the present moment through the use of your breath. Breathing slowly and comfortably can aid you in establishing a conscious presence; when doing this, you can let your breath be deep and gentle as there is no need to force it. Before starting your meditation practice, become aware of your breath and its tempo and depth. Once you are in tune with your breathing pattern, then you can begin to regulate the expanse of your breaths, consequently putting into effect the natural body's relaxation response.

Body Awareness

Body awareness is an excellent way of opening a meditative practice. You can do this by simply becoming aware of how your body comes in contact with the floor or with the surface underneath you. When doing this, try to feel the weight of your body and its overall sensation.

Moreover, as a way of gaining body awareness, you can also scan your body from the top of your head to the tip of your toes by bringing focus to each part of your body and the feeling that accompanies it. Furthermore, while practicing the meditations, it is of use to become aware of any stiffness or tightness in the face and body and, if present, acknowledge it and then release it. Tension tends to build up in some regions of the body, such as the jaw, neck, and shoulders. Giving these areas presence and acceptance through the breath can allow the tension to melt away and the muscles to relax.

Art Contemplation + Coloring

Coloring can be approached in a contemplative manner. To do this, bring awareness to how you are handling your pen or pencil, and if there is any tension in your hands, the wrist or fingers, just let it go. Hold your pen or pencil lightly and allow yourself to descend into the experience. If you would like to follow a more contemplative meditation, try to focus on the way the charcoal or the pencil or the ink of the pen pours into the paper. Lastly, you can empower your intention in this mediation by imagining by coloring the illustrations in the book you are sending or bathing the blessing subject with healing energy or with a specific healing color you are using to fill in the figure.

Relax into the Experience

Bring presence to your meditation by slowing down on each task. The point is not to finish the practice fast, but rather to come into the present moment. It is totally fine if your mind wanders. Thank or bless yourself for attempting to come into this space to relax, as this space is of yours to make.

Final Thoughts

This book is designed for both beginner and experienced meditators alike as the following active meditation exercises are easy to engage with and can be done anywhere and at any time. Active meditation is a practice that includes both breathing exercises and physical movement to reach a state of calm, presence, and clarity. This form of meditation offers many advantages in comparison with other passive techniques, such as seating meditation, since it is easier for the mind to quiet down when there is movement involved.

When meditating leave aside any judgments or expectations; a meditation session is neither good or bad, since the key to a rewarding mediation is enjoying the present moment. When you start to engage in this practice more and more, the beauty of the different experiences will surface, just as the ocean is beautifully different every single day of the year. Sometimes a meditation practice can bring something up, and sometimes it can be there, as it is, just as a practice.

Sometimes, part of the process of meditating is encountering resistance from the mind. This is because the human mind frequently tries to look away from the now and into habitual patterns based on future or past thinking. It is, however, a normal occurrence for the mind to question, challenge or resist new mental models, so becoming conscious of this resistance and then accepting questions as what they are, can open space for transformation to unfold.

When meditating, it can be helpful to become conscious of what thoughts, questions, or doubts may come up, and if it is of use to you, you can write them in a journal or in the journal section at the end of this book. Although it might not be for everyone, journaling can aid one in exploring if any blockages are keeping one from trusting one's words. For example, if one's blessing is "May I be there for myself" and the mind says, no way!, becoming conscious of this can shed light into one's mental processes, honing one's ability to observe the mind.

Through the use of simple mindfulness tools based on meditation practices and neuroplasticity findings on the power of meditation and gratitude, the following pages are set to empower you in rewiring your neural network through the use breath, intention, and coloring action.

Advice and Precautions

This book is not meant to diagnose, cure, or treat any disease. Only engage in these exercises as long as you feel comfortable. If you are pregnant or ill, consult with your doctor before initiating a breathwork technique. Remember to always listen to your body first. Do not practice these exercises while driving a car or operating any machinery. These exercises were specifically created for adults.

Self-Blessings Exercises

The following blessing exercises have been chosen based on their spiritual, and grounding strength. On the next pages, you will find a list of all the blessings material you will find in this book. At the end of all the appointed blessings, there will be space provided for you to articulate and practice your own self-blessing. For this exercise, use your intuition, creativity, and personal feeling to draft a blessing of your own.

As you follow the self-blessing exercises of this book, you will be able to facilitate you meditation by using the simple three-point process of:
- Breathing through presence
- Blessing through intention
- Embracing action through coloring.

1.   I recognize the human in me

2.   I acknowledge myself

        I thank myself

        I recognize myself

        I support myself

3.   I bless my existence

        I bless my presence

        I bless my being

        I bless myself

4.   May my thoughts be blessed

        May my feelings be blessed

        May my actions be blessed

        May my life be blessed

5.   May I believe in myself
        May I be there for myself
        May I honor myself
        May I bow to myself

6.   May my spirit be free
        May my body be free
        May my mind be free
        May I be free

7.   May my dreams be blessed
        May my inspiration be blessed
        May my vision be blessed
        May my intuition be blessed

8.   I bless my skin
        I bless my age
        I bless my path
        I bless myself

9.   I bless myself

10.   I bless my imperfections
        I bless my failings
        I bless my faults
        I bless my humanity

11. I bless my day
     I bless my morning
     I bless my afternoon
     I bless my night

12. May my inner child be happy
     May my inner child be free
     May my inner child be joyful
     May my inner child be protected

13. I welcome feeling safe
     I welcome feeling happy
     I welcome feeling at peace
     I welcome feeling loved

14. May I be with myself
     May I be for myself
     May I be connected with my needs
     May I be connected with myself

15. I bless my envy
     I bless my rage
     I bless my anger
     I bless my self-compassion

16. *A space for your personal blessing*

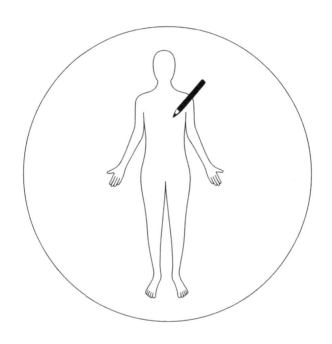

I recognize the human in me

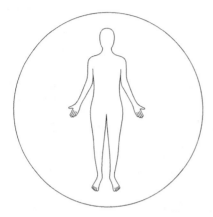

I recognize the human in me

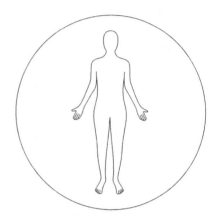

I recognize the human in me

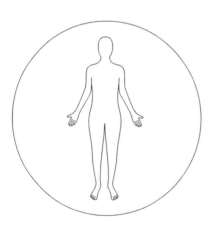

I recognize the human in me

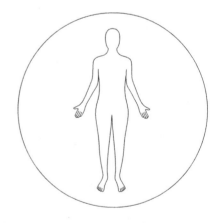

I recognize the human in me

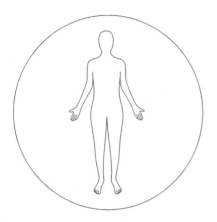

I recognize the human in me

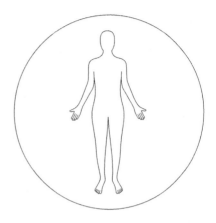

I recognize the human in me

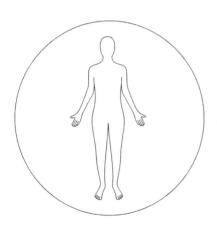

I recognize the human in me

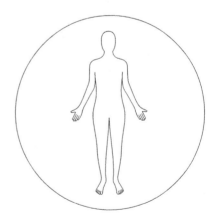

I recognize the human in me

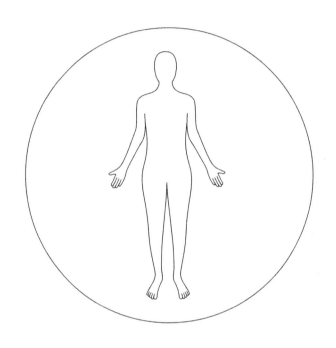

I acknowledge myself

I thank myself

I recognize myself

I support myself

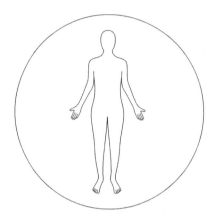

I acknowledge myself

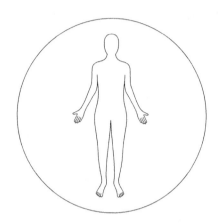

I thank myself

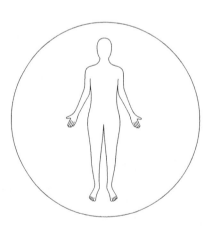

I recognize myself

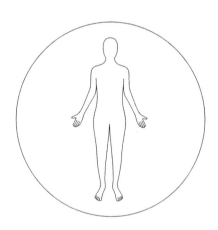

I support myself

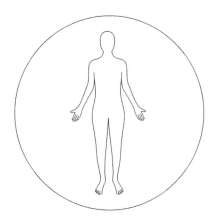

I acknowledge myself

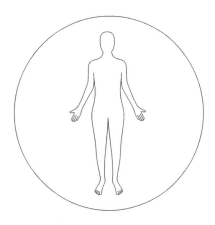

I thank myself

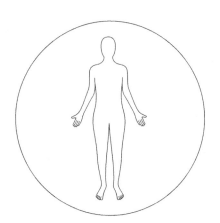

I recognize myself

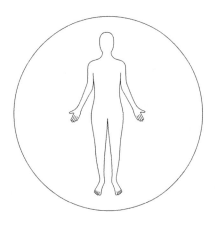

I support myself

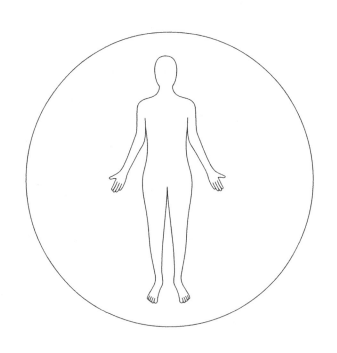

I bless my existence

I bless my presence

I bless my being

I bless myself

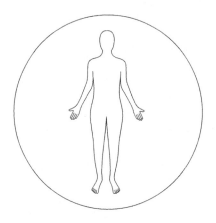

I bless my existence

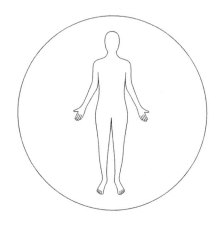

I bless my presence

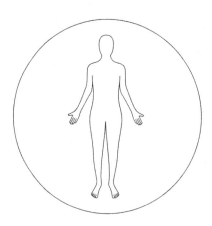

I bless my being

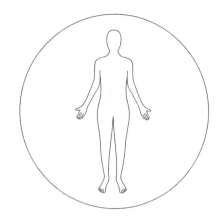

I bless myself

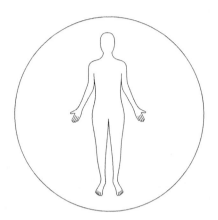

I bless my existence

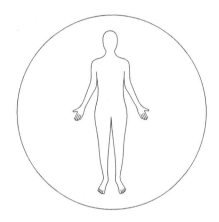

I bless my presence

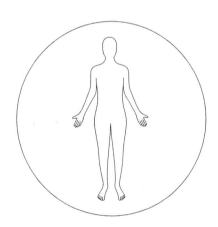

I bless my being

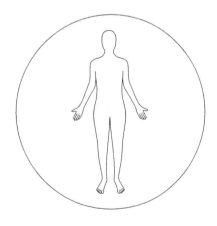

I bless myself

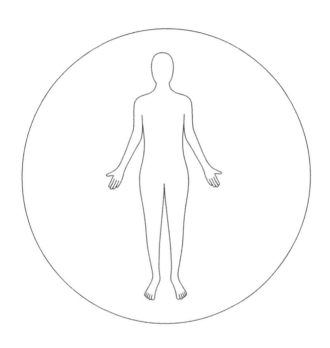

May my thoughts be blessed

May my feelings be blessed

May my actions be blessed

May my life be blessed

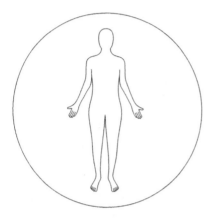

May my thoughts be blessed

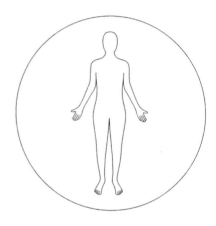

May my feelings be blessed

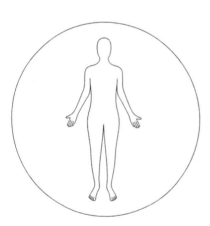

May my actions be blessed

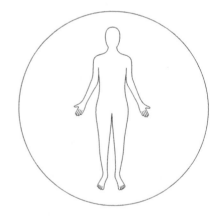

May my life be blessed

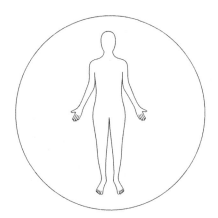

May my thoughts be blessed

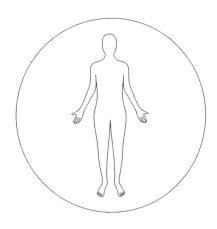

May my feelings be blessed

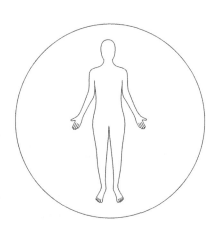

May my actions be blessed

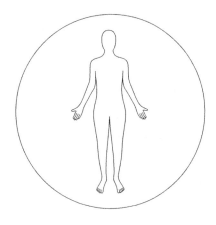

May my life be blessed

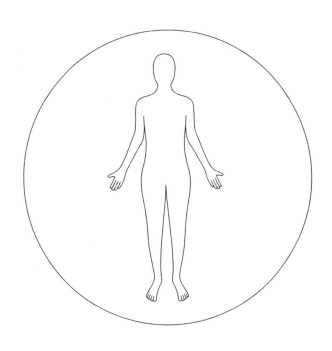

May I believe in myself

May I be there for myself

May I honor myself

May I bow to myself

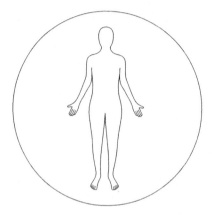

May I believe in myself

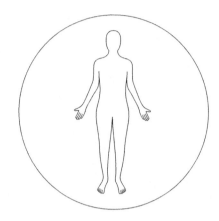

May I be there for myself

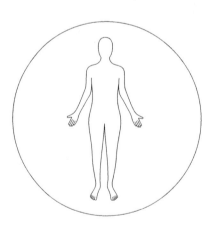

May I honor myself

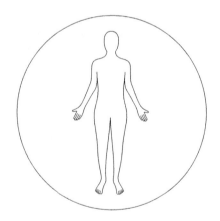

May I bow to myself

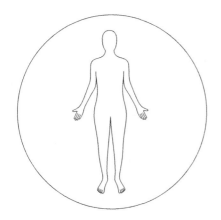

May I believe in myself

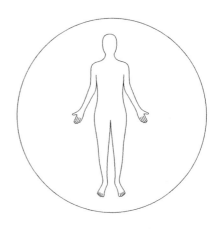

May I be there for myself

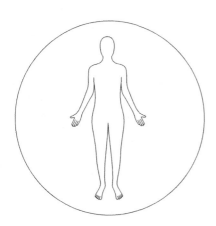

May I honor myself

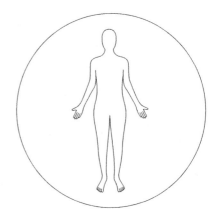

May I bow to myself

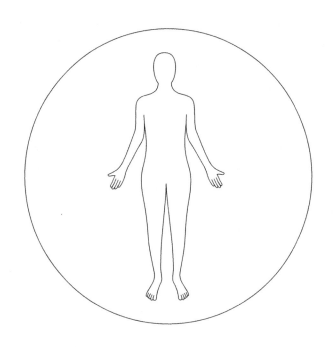

May my spirit be free

May my body be free

May my mind be free

May I be free

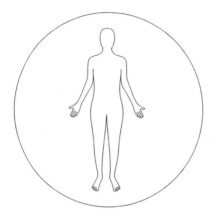

May my spirit be free

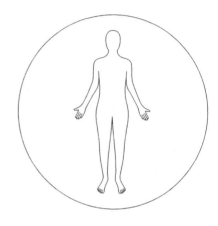

May my body be free

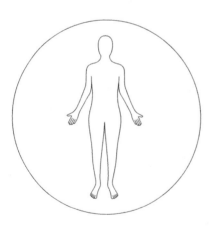

May my mind be free

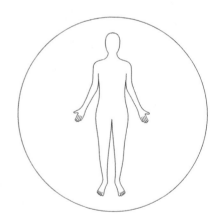

May I be free

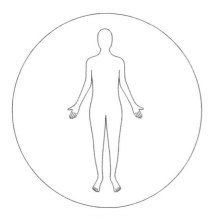

May my spirit be free

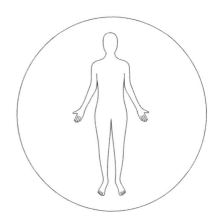

May my body be free

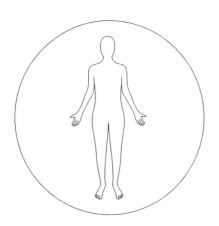

May my mind be free

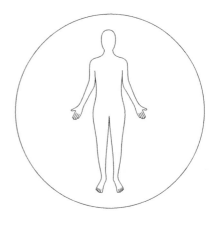

May I be free

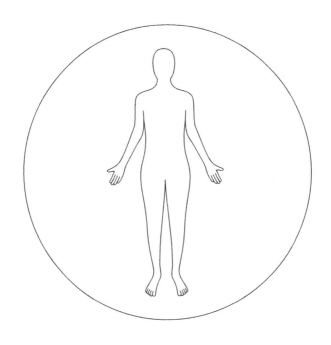

May my dreams be blessed

May my inspiration be blessed

May my vision be blessed

May my intuition be blessed

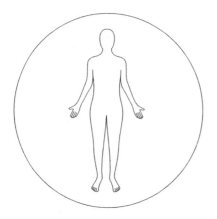

May my dreams be blessed

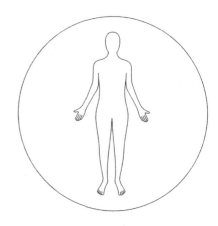

May my inspiration be blessed

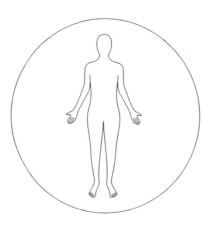

May my vision be blessed

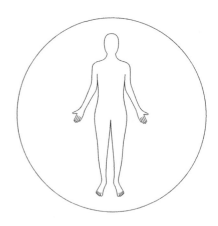

May my intuition be blessed

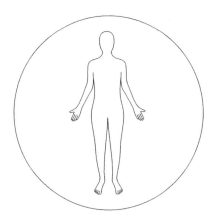

May my dreams be blessed

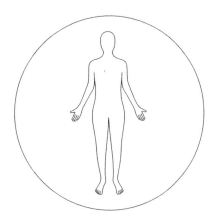

May my inspiration be blessed

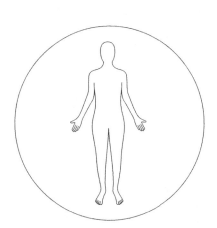

May my vision be blessed

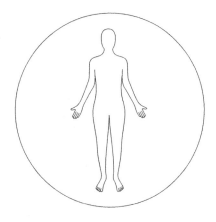

May my intuition be blessed

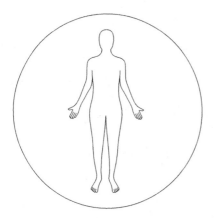

May my dreams be blessed

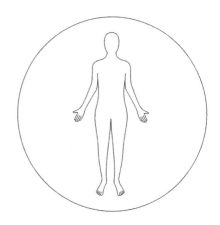

May my inspiration be blessed

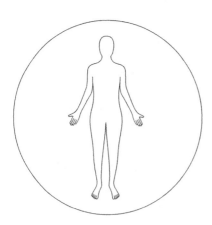

May my vision be blessed

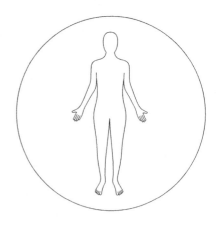

May my intuition be blessed

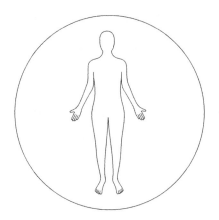

May my dreams be blessed

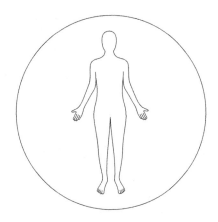

May my inspiration be blessed

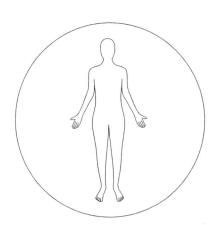

May my vision be blessed

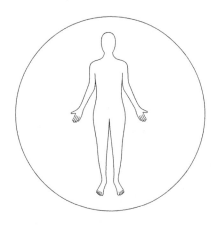

May my intuition be blessed

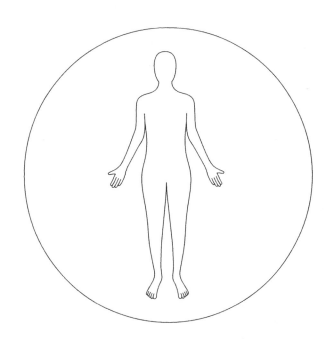

I bless my skin

I bless my age

I bless my path

I bless myself

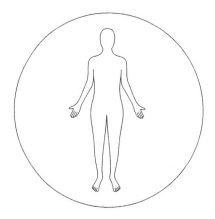

I bless my skin

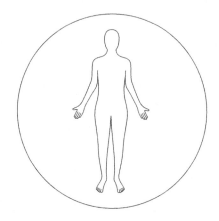

I bless my age

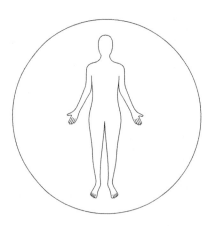

I bless my path

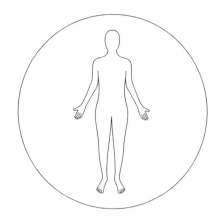

I bless myself

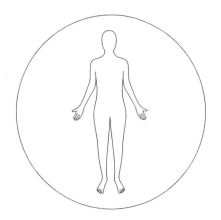

I bless my skin

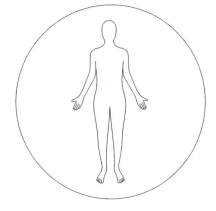

I bless my age

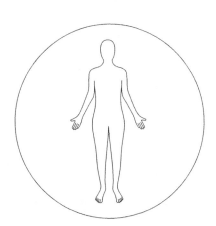

I bless my path

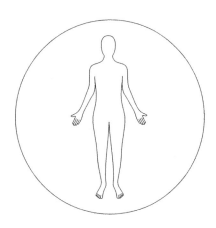

I bless myself

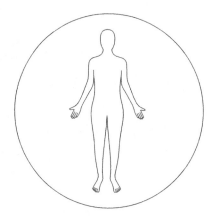

I bless my skin

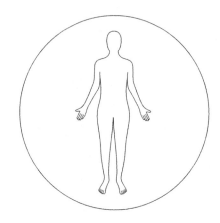

I bless my age

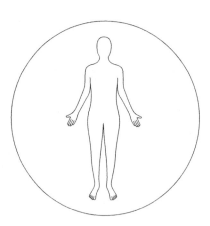

I bless my path

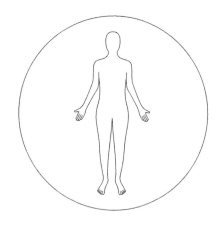

I bless myself

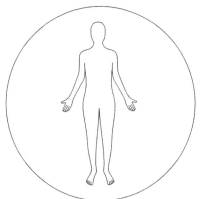

I bless my skin

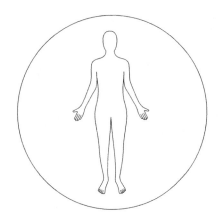

I bless my age

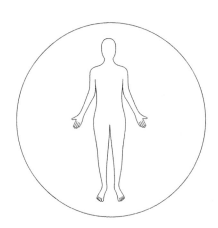

I bless my path

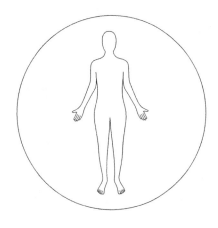

I bless myself

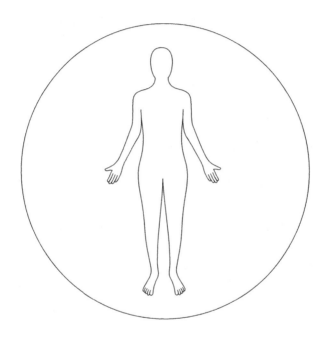

I bless myself

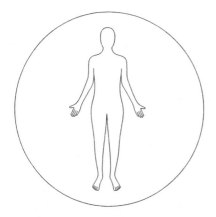

I bless myself

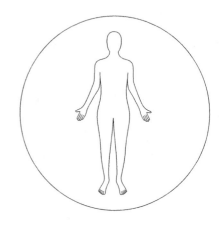

I bless myself

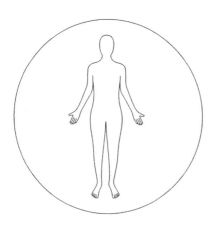

I bless myself

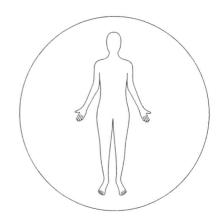

I bless myself

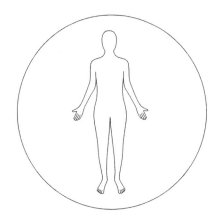

I bless myself

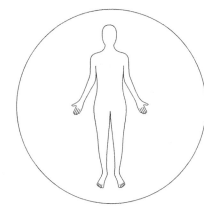

I bless myself

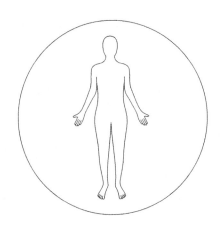

I bless myself

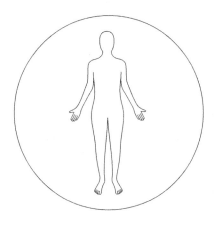

I bless myself

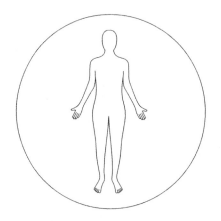

I bless myself

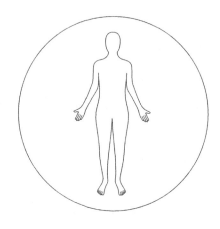

I bless myself

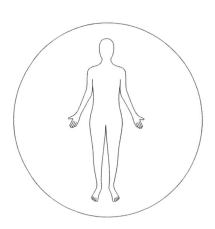

I bless myself

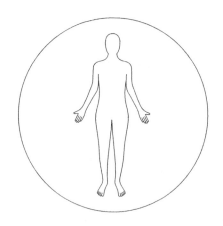

I bless myself

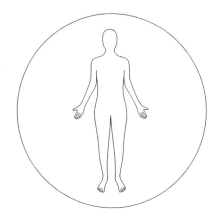

I bless myself

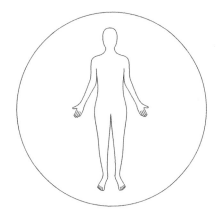

I bless myself

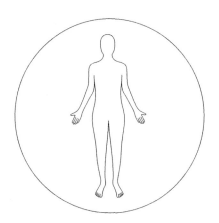

I bless myself

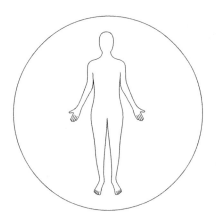

I bless myself

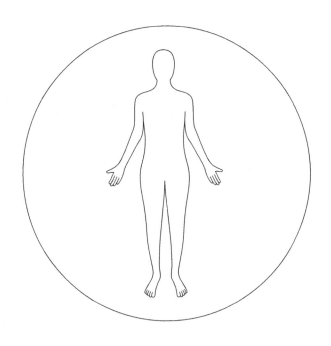

I bless my imperfections
I bless my failings
I bless my faults
I bless my humanity

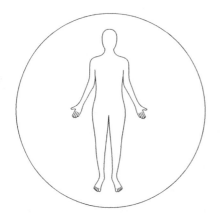

I bless my imperfections

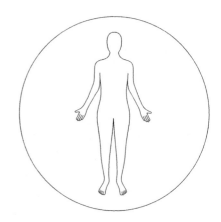

I bless my failings

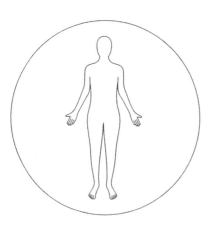

I bless my faults

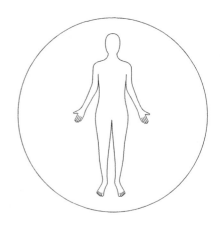

I bless my humanity

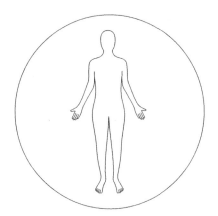

I bless my imperfections

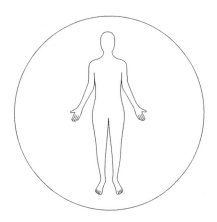

I bless my failings

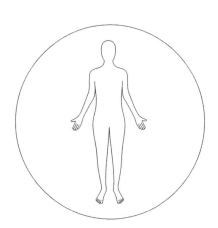

I bless my faults

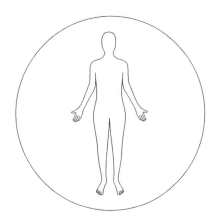

I bless my humanity

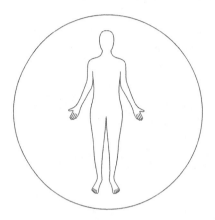

I bless my imperfections

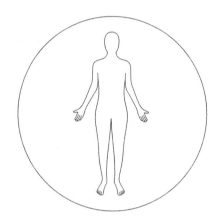

I bless my failings

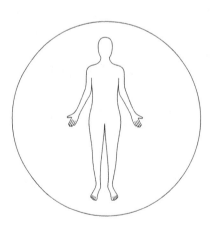

I bless my faults

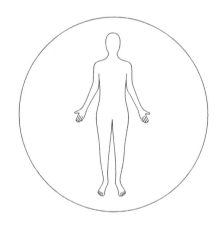

I bless my humanity

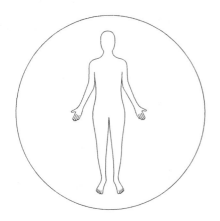

I bless my imperfections

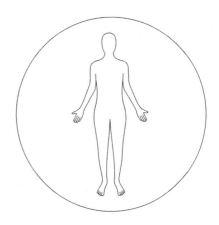

I bless my failings

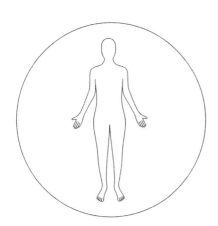

I bless my faults

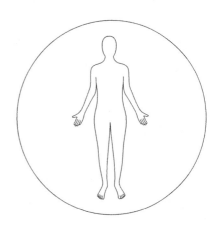

I bless my humanity

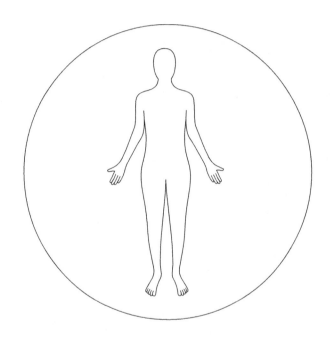

I bless my day
I bless my morning
I bless my afternoon
I bless my night

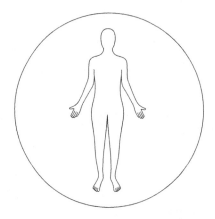

I bless my day

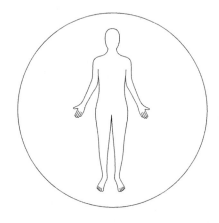

I bless my morning

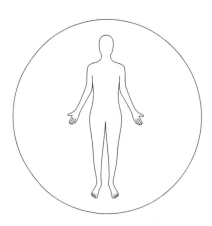

I bless my afternoon

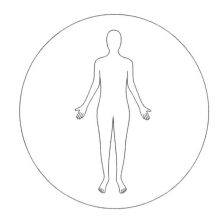

I bless my night

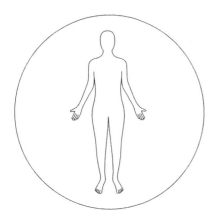

I bless my day

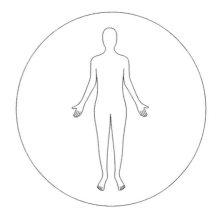

I bless my morning

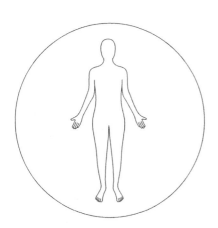

I bless my afternoon

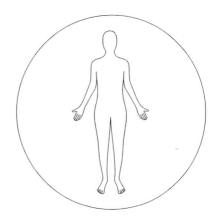

I bless my night

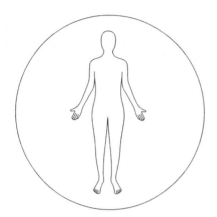

I bless my day

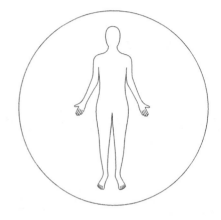

I bless my morning

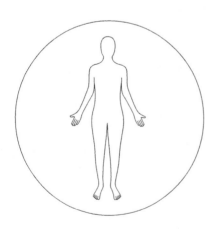

I bless my afternoon

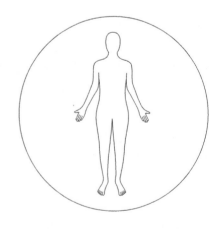

I bless my night

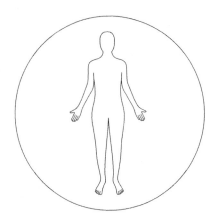

I bless my day

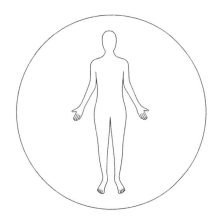

I bless my morning

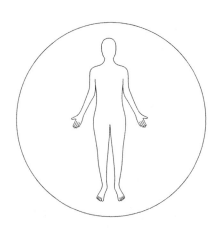

I bless my afternoon

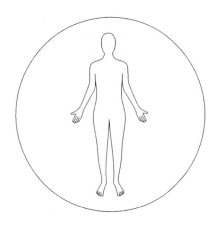

I bless my night

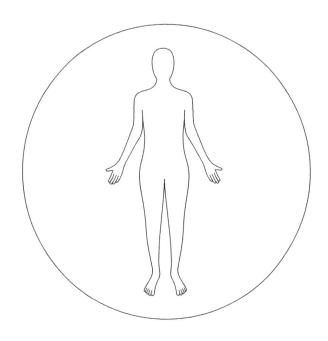

May my inner child be happy
May my inner child be free
May my inner child be joyful
May my inner child be protected

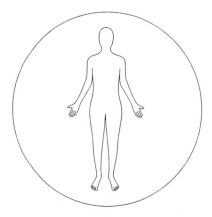

May my inner child be happy

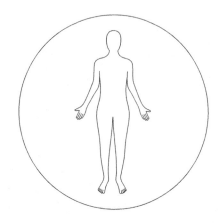

May my inner child be free

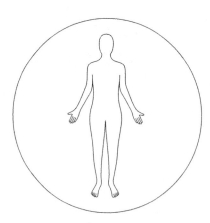

May my inner child be joyful

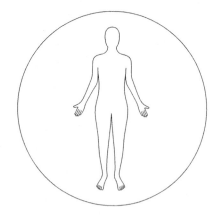

May my inner child be protected

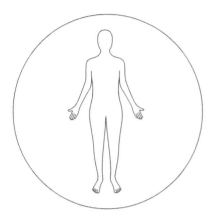

May my inner child be happy

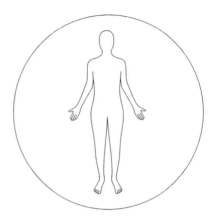

May my inner child be free

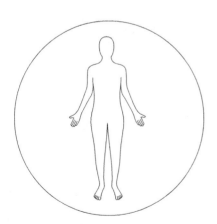

May my inner child be joyful

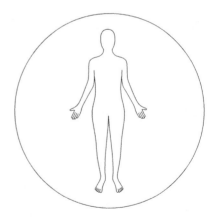

May my inner child be protected

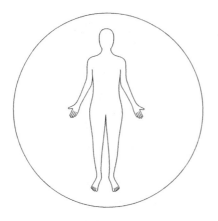

May my inner child be happy

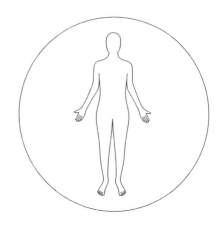

May my inner child be free

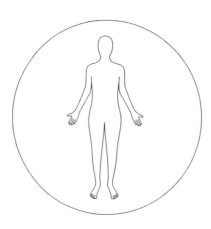

May my inner child be joyful

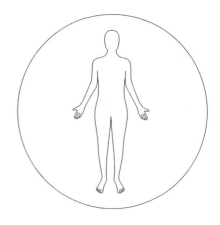

May my inner child be protected

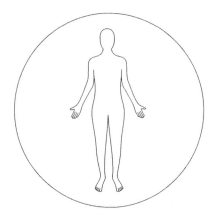

May my inner child be happy

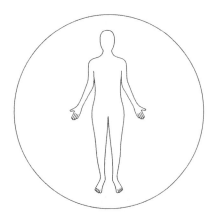

May my inner child be free

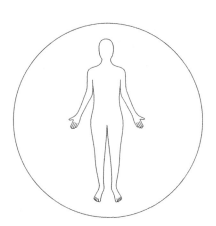

May my inner child be joyful

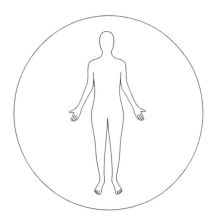

May my inner child be protected

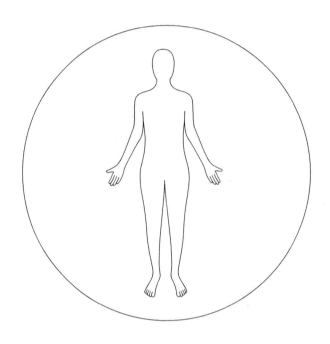

I welcome feeling safe

I welcome feeling happy

I welcome feeling at peace

I welcome feeling loved

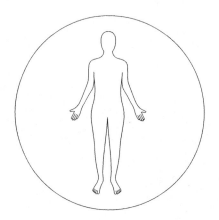

I welcome feeling safe

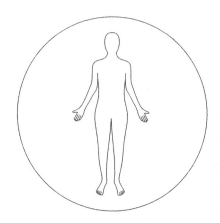

I welcome feeling happy

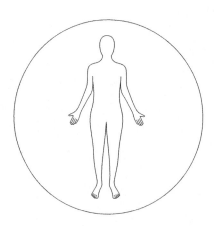

I welcome feeling at peace

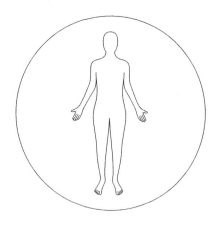

I welcome feeling loved

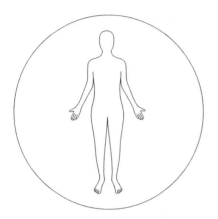

I welcome feeling safe

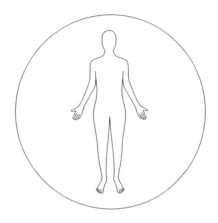

I welcome feeling happy

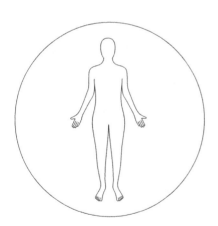

I welcome feeling at peace

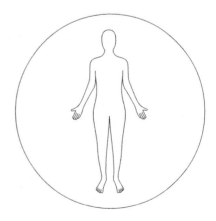

I welcome feeling loved

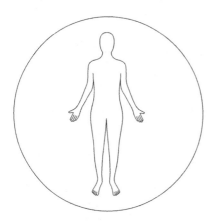

I welcome feeling safe

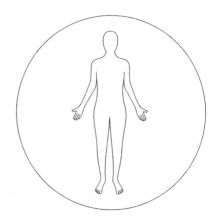

I welcome feeling happy

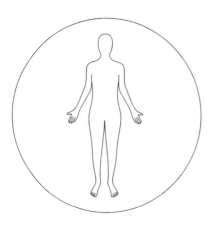

I welcome feeling at peace

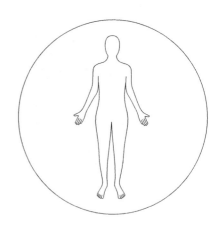

I welcome feeling loved

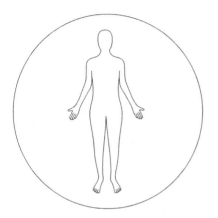

I welcome feeling safe

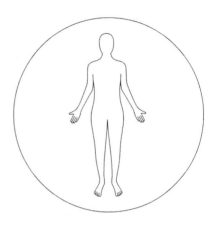

I welcome feeling happy

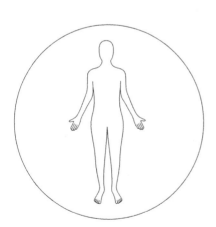

I welcome feeling at peace

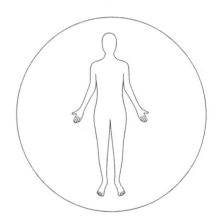

I welcome feeling loved

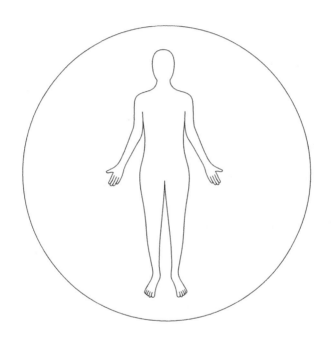

May I be with myself

May I be for myself

May I be connected with my needs

May I be connected with myself

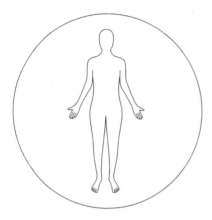

May I be with myself

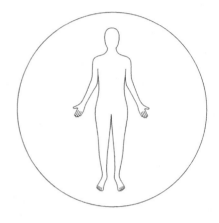

May I be for myself

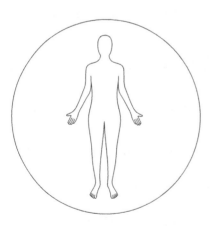

May I be connected with my needs

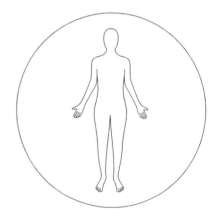

May I be connected with myself

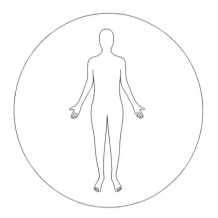

May I be with myself

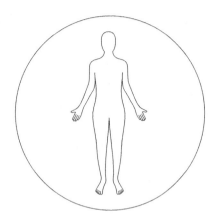

May I be for myself

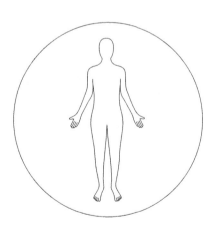

May I be connected with my needs

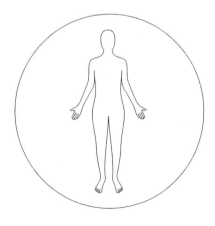

May I be connected with myself

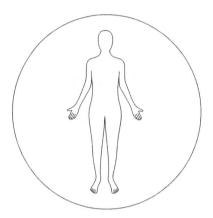

May I be with myself

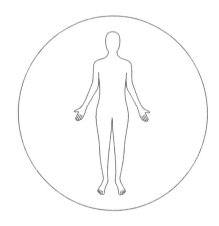

May I be for myself

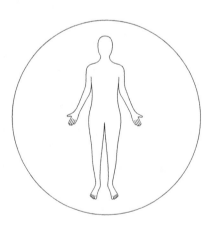

May I be connected with my needs

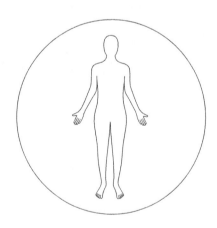

May I be connected with myself

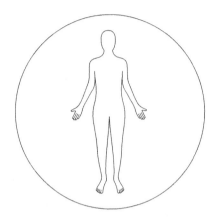

May I be with myself

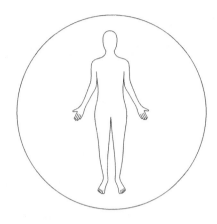

May I be for myself

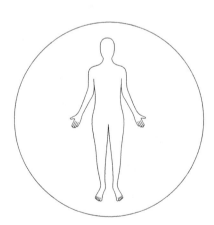

May I be connected with my needs

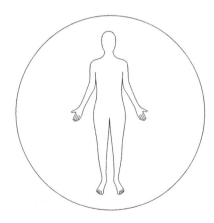

May I be connected with myself

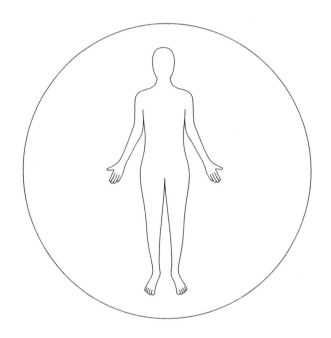

I bless my envy

I bless my rage

I bless my anger

I bless my self-compassion

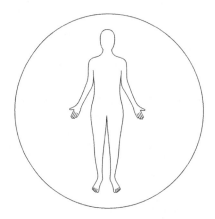

I bless my envy

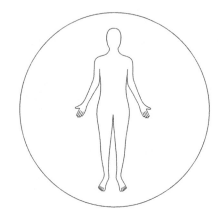

I bless my rage

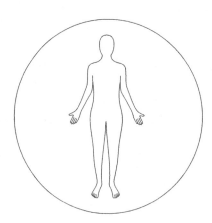

I bless my anger

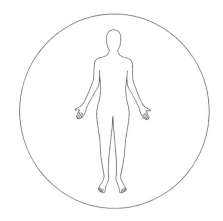

I bless my self-compassion

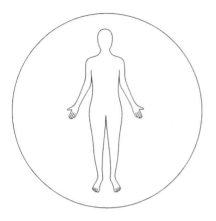

I bless my envy

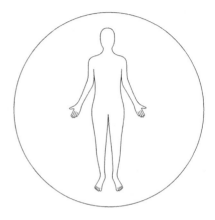

I bless my rage

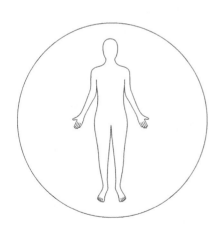

I bless my anger

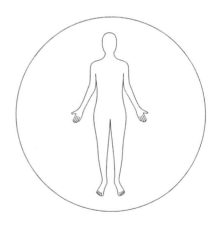

I bless my self-compassion

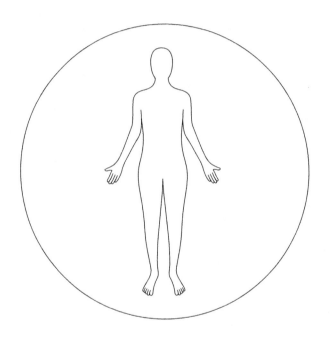

a space for you personal blessing:

_____

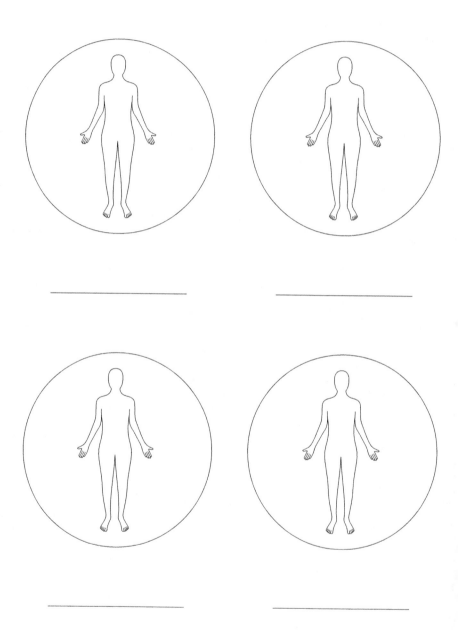

_____   _____

_____   _____

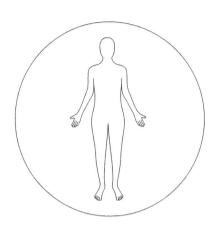

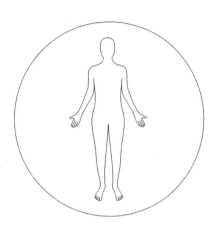

_____   _____

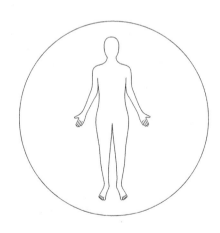

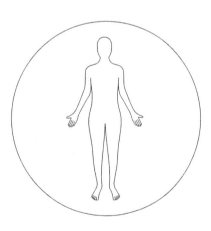

_____   _____

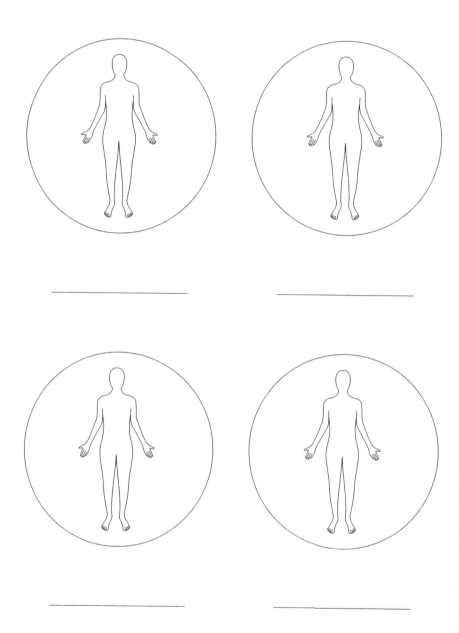

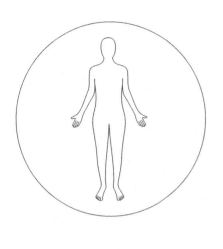

_____

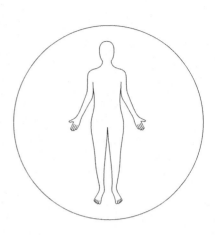

_____

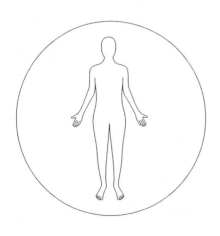

_____

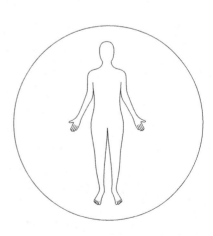

_____

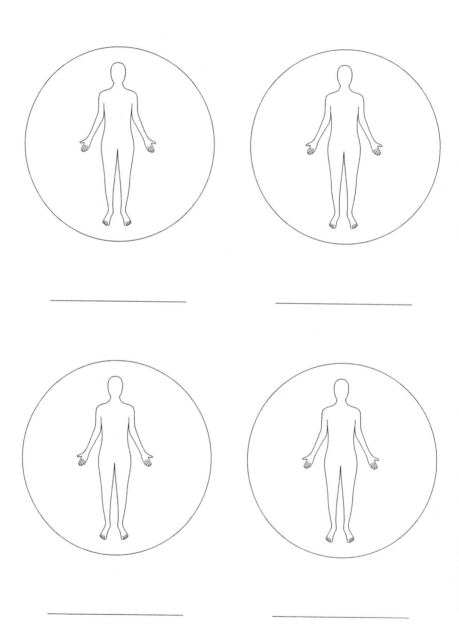

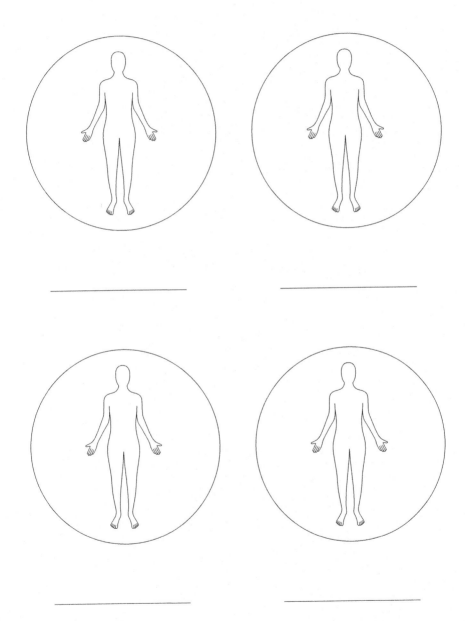

_____   _____

_____   _____

Journal

Journal

Journal

Journal

Journal

Journal

Journal

Journal

Journal

Endnotes

1. *Counting Blessings Versus Burdens: An Experimental Investigation of Gratitude and Subjective Well-Being in Daily Life.* Robert A. Emmons and Michael E. McCullough. Journal of Personality and Social Psychology. 2003

2. *In Praise of Gratitude.* Harvard Health Publishing. Harvard Medical School. 2019

3. *In Praise of Gratitude.* Harvard Health Publishing. Harvard Medical School. 2019

4. *Positive Outlook Speeds Recovery.* Harvard Health Publishing. Harvard Medical School. 2013.

5. *Counting Blessings Versus Burdens.* Robert A. Emmons and Michael E. McCullough. Journal of Personality and Social Psychology. 2003

6. *What is Loving-Kindness Meditation?.* Madhuleena Roy Chowdhury. Positive Psychology. 2019.

7. *Happiness: Essential Mindfulness Practices.* Thich Nhat Hanh. 2009

+ Research Articles

1. *Open hearts build lives: positive emotions, induced through loving-kindness meditation, build consequential personal resources.* Fredrickson, Cohn, Coffey, Pek & Finkel. 2008.

2. *Loving-kindness and compassion meditation: potential for psychological interventions.* Hofman SG, Grossman P, Hinton DE. 2011.

3. *How positive emotions build physical health: perceived positive social connections account for the upward spiral between positive emotions and vagal tone.* Kok BE, Coffey KA, Cohn MA, Catalino Li, Vacharkulksemsuk T, Brantley M, Fredrikson BL. 2013.

4. *Loving-kindness meditation for chronic low back pain: results from a pilot trial.* Carson JW, Keefe FJ, Lynch TR, Carson Km, Goli V, Fras AM, Thorp SR. 2005.

5. *Meditation-based treatment yielding immediate relief for meditation-naïve migraineurs.* Tonelli ME, Wachholtz AB. 2014.

6. *Distinct neural activity associated with focused-attention meditation and loving-kindness meditation.* Lee TM, Leung MK, Hou WK, Tang JC, Yin J, So KF, Lee CF, Chan CC. 2012.

Acknowledgements

I would first like to thank you Rune from Bornholm, your heart-filled presence always moves me at the sight of so much understanding, compassion and love. Amelie, Amelia, Ameluki, Amelao, you are the joy of my every morning, my soft pillow, my daily hot chocolate, my embrace. All my dance teachers, shamans, spiritual guides, the Amsterdam parrots and the crows, the grasshopper strength, nature and the seasons, thank you. The trees from Westerpark who provide so much nurture, thank you. The little hill next to the labyrinth, thank you. And all of you who have assured me, that doing a project like this is worth it. Leonie Evita, Alek Binek, Karen Guzman, Susan, Yoko and Rachel thank you for your presence in my life. I thank you, I thank you, I thank you. May all the blessings be with you. May all the blessings be with you. May all the blessings be with you.

About the Author

Karenina Ana Murillo is the founder of the Coloring Method, bridging mindfulness and art through the publication of art therapy workbooks, mindfulness guides, coloring books, meditation manuals, breathwork visualizations, gratitude journals and more. Her engagement as an art librarian and artist at the Arts Students League, New York and Greenwich Pottery House, New York, led her to explore creative expressions as an avenue for finding presence through the arts of contemplation. Delving into meditative practices through the crevices of art led Karen to connect with art as a poetic form of bringing together the present moment and art through the creation of the Coloring Method.

Karenina Ana Murillo is a Certified Yoga Teacher, Sociologist, Culture Anthropologist, and Artist (BA, MA). She has studied at the Arts Students League of New York, University of Vienna and Cal Arts.

Cover Photo by Angel Origgi

More Book Titles and Series

RETURNING TO THE BREATH SERIES

Guide 1
Guide 2
Guide 3
Guide 4
Guide 5
Guide 6
Guide 7
Guide 8
Guide 9
Guide 10

PRANAYAMA SERIES

Step Stair Breath
Viloma Krama
Alternate Nostril
Visualizing Prana
4.7.8 Breath
Equal Ratio Breath
Ujjayi Breath
Cooling Breath
Hissing Breath
Floating Breath
Right Nostril Breathing
Left Nostril Breath
Bee Breath
Bellows Breath
Breath of Fire
Om Meditation
So Ham Meditation

I AM SERIES

I am aware
I am here
I am safe
I am peace
I am relaxed
I am alive
I am fulfilled
I am sincere
I am life
I am beautiful
I am clarity

THERE IS SERIES

There is peace
There is love
There is understanding
There is connection
There is collaboration
There is hope
There is reason
There is sense
There is listening
There is time
There is space
There is meaning
There is genuineness
There is silence
There is life
There is wisdom
There is consciousness

SPIRITUAL SERIES

I am sacred
I am human
I am flow
I am nature
I am light
I am awakened
I believe
I belong
I am love
I am centered
I am aligned
I am flow
I have flow
I am warmness
I am there
I am breath
I am healed
I am life
I am sustenance
I am the journey
I am connected
I am magic
I am energy

YOGA MANTRA SERIES

Om
Om Shanti
Chakras

Made in the USA
Columbia, SC
25 June 2020